lonely planet

50

Bars

TO BLOW YOUR MIND

Contents

Introduction

The best bars are much more than the sum of their parts. The various components, like great service, smart design, spectacular views and perfect cocktails, merge to create one joyous drinking experience. It's not always easy to put your finger on the moment when mind-blowing is achieved, but you sure know when it happens. Mid-quaff, you realise you're happy. You look around you and realise you're having the kind of time you just know you'll be telling people about. Probably while you're still there.

But how have we whittled down this list? Well, some bars have earned their spot by playing up their obvious assets, whether it's an interesting urban location or a stunning natural setting. Others are champions of the basics, be they cocktails or single liquors, while still others do something dramatically unusual or fun; some are so quirky it's impossible not to marvel over a custom-made cocktail. But perhaps the secret sauce in all this is genuine desire to delight each drinker, guest or customer who walks through the door. (Or crawls through a tunnel, takes a glass lift or lounges on a deck chair.) It's a love of hospitality and an enthusiasm for the precious drop.

Whether you're a fan of barefoot, surfside imbibing or you prefer sophisticated cocktails in stylish surrounds, it's time to plan your list. Life is short. Cheers, salut, bottoms up. See you at the bar.

Wow factor // Beautiful bars

BAB AL SHAMS, AL QUDRA RD,
DUBAI, UNITED ARAB EMIRATES
WWW.MEYDANHOTELS.COM/BABALSHAMS

Al Sarab / Dubai

THIS IS NOT THE DESERT.
Maybe not, but you're surrounded by it. As is the exclusive Bab Al Shams Desert Resort and Spa, which is exactly where you are right now.

WHY GO HERE? WE'RE AFTER A DRINK...
It's true that UAE is a dry country but inside the walls of this luxury resort there are exceptions, and one important exception is the Al Sarab. Consider it your very own oasis.

I'M GUESSING THAT THIS ISN'T GOING TO BE A DIVE BAR.
You guessed right. Dubai is renowned for luxury and extravagance and the Al Sarab doesn't disappoint. This two-storey rooftop bar overlooks the Arabian Desert and is spotted with semi-private banquettes, laden with cushions and lit by soft lantern light. There'll be a gentle breeze coming in from the desert and, to complete the scene, melodious oud music playing softly in the background. You are now set for a very memorable evening.

IT SOUNDS LIKE A TRANSCENDENT EXPERIENCE.
A couple of the bar's signature 'Desert Classic' cocktails ordered to the table and a few puffs of the tableside shisha (a gamut of fruit-inspired varieties available) can pretty much guarantee it.

The Island Bar / Sydney

I'M GUESSING THIS IS MORE THAN A BIG BENCH IN THE MIDDLE OF A ROOM?

Spot on. Cockatoo Island is the location, smack bang in the middle of Sydney's harbour.

THE VIEW MUST BE SPECIAL.

Its views are everything you want to see when in Sydney. Plus, you can take it all in on a deck chair under a striped beach umbrella with a cocktail and a slice of wood-fired pizza.

SOUNDS PRETTY IDYLLIC.

It does now but it wasn't always so rosy on Cockatoo Island; in the 19th century the island was used to house convicts who had reoffended in the colony.

I'M INNOCENT!

Luckily for modern patrons the island is a short ferry ride to and from the mainland and is decidedly more comfortable than it once was. That said, the island is still at the mercy of the elements – the bar is sometimes forced to close when the sea is too threatening and shuts in winter. The rest of the time the converted-shipping-container bar pumps out tropically themed cocktail creations like the Captain Thunderbolt Mai Tai (named after the only prisoner to escape the island).

Northern Lights / Reykjavik

A CHRISTMAS-THEMED BAR?
Not a chance. This is Nordic uber-cool boutique bar action, about 45 minutes' drive from Reykjavik.

WILL I SEE THE AURORA BOREALIS?
May to October is the best time for some dazzling light shows. The double-height windows look out across the ice-worn rocks and barren ground with a full sky backdrop. If your vision was up to it, you could probably see forever.

THAT SOUNDS PRETTY SPECIAL.
There's no question, this place is all about location, location,

location. As a part of the Ion Luxury Adventure Hotel, you'll find a quality drink (though you may have to call for service in this minimalist-in-all-ways establishment).

SO I'VE SEEN THE LIGHTS. NOW WHAT?
If it can be called adventure, you can do it here: hiking volcanoes, horse riding on black-sand beaches, super-jeeping to glaciers and waterfalls. And more: rafting, fissure diving, ice climbing. You'll be seeing stars. Or lights, anyway.

DO I HAVE TO DO ALL THAT?
Yes. Yes, you do.

118TH FL, INTERNATIONAL COMMERCE CENTRE,
1 AUSTIN ROAD WEST, HONG KONG, CHINA
WWW.RITZCARLTON.COM/EN

Ozone Bar / Hong Kong

FUNNY NAME FOR A BAR.

Well, there are many contenders for that title, surely! And when you're on the 118th floor looking down, you'll feel like you're somewhere in the ozone layer 15km up.

ISN'T OZONE BAD FOR ME?

You'll be fine, you won't be breathing it! Instead you'll be drinking some of the finest cocktails in Asia.

HMMM. REALLY? A HOTEL BAR?

If you're in Hong Kong, you'd be crazy not to pay a visit, if only for the view. Factor in seriously well-made, unique house-devised wonders in a luxe, stylish cloud in the sky and it'll be the best $30 you spend!

$30 FOR A DRINK!!!

A trip to the building's observation deck is about $20, so depending on your priorities, this is potentially a bargain. You can spend less than that, but why not spoil yourself?

OK, I'M IN. WHAT DO I ORDER?

Have a 'Dragontini'...you might see Drogon flying by. It's a vodka-based cocktail with raspberry, yuzu and basil accents – it's sure to help with your urge to soar.

63RD FL, STATE TOWER,
1055 TH SILOM, BANGKOK, THAILAND
WWW.LEBUA.COM/SKY-BAR

Sky Bar / Bangkok

SO WHERE IS THIS PLACE?
Halfway between Bangkok and earth's exosphere, 63 floors up on the roof of the luxury Lebua State Tower.

WHY AM I HERE?
Pollution-free alfresco cocktails with Bangkok's style-set and a 360° view of the frenetic, sprawling beast of a city below.

AM I REALLY IN BANGKOK? IT COULD BE LA.
True, there is something LA about Sky Bar's gaudy, incongruous architectural styles, with its Greco-Roman columns and enormous golden dome, but that's all part of the fun. Plus, the punters aren't all fans of *The Hangover II* (which featured the bar in some scenes).

I'M FEELING A LITTLE DIZZY.
Vertigo sufferers: hug the sides and send a heights-immune friend to the psychedelic circular bar. It hovers, spaceship-like, over the skyline, pulsing with different colours. Hopefully they'll come back with the bar's signature drink, a Sunset 63.

A COUPLE OF SUNSET 63S DOWN, FOOD PLEASE.
Head down the stone steps to the garden terraces, where peckish punters satiate on light, Mediterranean-inspired fare.

Water and Wind Bar / Binh Duong

IT'S SOUNDING VERY ELEMENTAL.
You'll be blown away.

HA. COME ON, WHY AM I HERE?
There is no bar like this on the planet. Just look at it. The magnificent structure is made entirely of thatch and bamboo and uses the natural breezes and cool water from the lake on which it is situated to create natural ventilation.

KEEP TALKING.
From the outside it looks like an enormous, hairy dome floating on a still lake; on the inside the intricate criss-crossing of the bamboo branches are entirely exposed, and the cathedral-like height of the ceiling features an opening to the sky. Lamps, chairs and tables and the bar itself are also made exclusively from bamboo – the result is a warm and tropical vibe.

IT'S AMAZING. NOW WHAT ABOUT THE DRINKING?
Ummm, look at the sunlight casting a warm glow on the bamboo walls, or the shimmery reflection coming off the water through the low windows – what we're trying to say here is that food and drink isn't what makes this place special. There's a classic selection of alcohol on offer and a small menu of Southeast Asian snacks.

16TH FL, BLDG 3,
MOSCOW, RUSSIA
WWW.WHITERABBITMOSCOW.COM

White Rabbit / Moscow

DOWN THE RABBIT HOLE?

The White Rabbit has been racking up the accolades over the years for its incredible food and regularly makes it to lists of best restaurants in the world. Good news for booze hounds! You'll find that it is possible to sample both the hospitality and the spectacular space in the Moscovian setup without blowing the budget on a full meal.

WHAT MAKES THE SETTING SO SPECTACULAR?

The bar/restaurant is 16 floors up on the Smolensky Passage and is encased entirely in glass, like a gigantic greenhouse.

The result of the glass cover is a stunning 360° view of the sprawling city. The seating is mostly made up of large, opulent couches piled with comfy cushions, making it super easy to keep ordering delicious drinks like the Drunk Bumblebee – vodka, limoncello, basil, pineapple, lemon and sugar syrup.

THE FOOD DOES LOOK PRETTY TEMPTING.

If a full degustation is out of your league the White Rabbit has recently opened the Gastrobar, an opportunity for guests to sit and chat with chefs and bartenders as they make paired drinks and dishes.

Mixology // Cocktail bars

Academia da Cachaça /
Rio De Janeiro

IS THIS A UNIVERSITY?
You are about to be schooled in the fine art of cachaça, the Brazilian national spirit, and your caipirinha will never be the same again. You'll also get a good lesson or two in traditional Brazilian cuisine.

THIS IS MY KIND OF SCHOOL.
This is a bar that sets out to celebrate and illuminate its roots, but the worthy endeavour won't stop you having good time.

I THINK I NEED A PRIMER ON CACHAÇA.
The drink is a sugarcane spirit, like rum, but distilled from pure sugarcane juice rather than from molasses. It brings on an earthier taste, and when the folk at Academia da Cachaça take it and blend it into a cocktail (you have to try out an authentic caipirinha: lime, sugar and cachaça muddled into a fresh, palate-exploding elixir), you'll feel like you've just graduated.

I'D LIKE TO DO A PHD PLEASE.
Be their guests. The traditional Brazilian cuisine (the *feijoada* – the Brazilian national dish of beans and meat – served here is considered a lesson to all others) will keep you strong through those long hours of study.

134 ELDRIDGE ST,
NEW YORK CITY, USA

Attaboy / New York City

I♥NYC.
You are not the first. Here's another reason to do so: Attaboy.

WHAT COULD POSSIBLY MAKE MY LOVE GROW?
Some bars make it to these best lists because they're spectacularly designed, some are in spectacular locations, some are quirky and bizarre and some earn their place at the top of the pile by getting the simple things just right. Attaboy is such a place.

SO NO BELLS AND WHISTLES THEN?
It's not that Attaboy doesn't have a nice speakeasy-style fit-out, it does – the exposed and whitewashed brick walls are cosy and the long wooden and brushed steel bar is polished and inviting. The almost-hidden Chinatown locale and the knock-and-buzz entry system lends an air of exclusivity which is always intriguing. However, the real magic at this place is in the drinks and the suspender-clad geniuses mixing them.

SIGNATURE COCKTAILS PERHAPS?
None in sight, in fact there's no cocktail menu: it's all about bespoke concoctions. Give the bartender some favourite flavours or tell him how you're feeling and he'll create a drink from scratch that matches your cravings and your mood.

© ATTABOY

ANNIVERSARY BUILDING IF,
1-6-4 AZABU-JUBAN, MINATO-KU, TOKYO, JAPAN
WWW.GENYAMAMOTO.JP

Gen Yamamoto / Tokyo

THIS PLACE IS TINY!

There are just eight seats at the L-shaped oak wood bar and only New York trained mixologist Gen Yamamoto behind it.

IT'S MAKING ME FEEL SPECIAL JUST THINKING ABOUT IT.

For every lucky patron Gen creates a cocktail tasting menu like no other (you can also buy individual drinks). Working within the ethos of Japanese 'shiki', Gen adheres to the freshness and seasonality of ingredients while building a harmonious sequence of flavours. He crafts cocktails like a sushi master, all deliberate strokes and minimum movement.

WHAT DOES A GEN COCKTAIL LOOK LIKE?

A sample of components used may include gin with crushed Shizuoka tomatoes and a single shiso leaf, or shochu (a Japanese spirit) with cooked and raw kumquats and cubed daikon. Gen focusses on flavour as well as textural elements and temperatures which he expertly balances in order to create a sensory experience for the lucky quaffer. The whole thing feels exclusive, exquisite and quintessentially Japanese.

WITH ONLY EIGHT SEATS – HOW DO I GET IN?

Reservations are highly recommended, but it's open from 3pm so if you haven't booked, get in early and hope for the best.

VESTERBROGADE 72B,
COPENHAGEN, DENMARK
WWW.LIDKOEB.DK

Lidkoeb / Copenhagen

IS THIS A SCANDI CRIME-SCENE THEMED BAR?
Move along, detective.

WHY GO THERE?
For the garish décor, boisterous crowd, cheap eats...just kidding; in fact, a shiver just went down the spine of every Dane at the very thought. Lidkoeb is the opposite of gauche; it is the epitome of mid-century style. The ground floor (one of three that the bar occupies) is spacious and white and features tan leather banquettes, draped with shaggy furs. At one end there's a giant hearth with raging fire, flanked by more stylish leather seating and giant exposed beams. The bar itself is tiled in white and topped with a warm blonde wood. Altogether, there's style and sophistication in spades.

GREAT, SO I'VE ENDED UP AT A DANISH DESIGN FAIR.
Despite the meticulous attention to detail, there's still love and respect for service and for fine cocktails, like the 'Lille Fortun' – Tanqueray gin, Chartreuse Verte, fresh lemon, sugar, house pale ale and fresh sage leaves.

OK, THIS IS PICKING UP.
Bar snacks like the Comte with quince jam are flawless in their simplicity, like the perfect crime.

BUDAPESTER STRASSE 40,
BERLIN, GERMANY
WWW.25HOURS-HOTEL.COM

Monkey Bar / Berlin

I'M HERE BECAUSE ...?
Because monkeys.

REALLY?
Well, maybe not just because you can see all the monkey business going on in the primate enclosure of the Berlin Zoo below... It's also a great place to see the sun set against sweeping views of Berlin's buzzing city streets.

WHAT'S IT LIKE INSIDE?
There's a semi-industrial-meets-animal-safari feel to the Monkey Bar with its exposed steel beams and a large, square, black bar overhung by apothecary-bottle drop lamps. The hard lines are warmed up by the use of soft furnishings like the blue, red and yellow leather ottomans, tapestried throw cushions, tree-trunk stools and living plants. There's a wrap-around outdoor terrace with loungy seating that gets packed on sunny summer days.

WHAT SHOULD I DRINK?
It's a toss-up between the 'King Kong' – Guatemalan vanilla rum, sugar syrup, chocolate spirits and cherry bitters, and the 'Ape's Twist' – vodka, elderflower liqueur, cloudy apple juice, lemon juice and soda water.

650 GOUGH ST,
SAN FRANCISCO, USA
WWW.SMUGGLERSCOVESF.COM

Smuggler's Cove / San Francisco

ISN'T THERE A MOVIE ABOUT THIS?
Once you visit it will be on the silver screen of your memory for years to come.

THAT'S A BIG-TICKET PROMISE!
Doesn't everyone dream of being shipwrecked off the Caribbean coast in a 17th-century brig loaded with alcohol meant for the New World?

SO I CAN EXPECT A BUCCANEERING CROWD SWIGGING RUM BY THE GALLON?
Despite the nautical ropes, carved mermaids and even a waterfall, this is no tacky bar. Smuggler's Cove is serious when it comes to alcohol, especially its beloved rum. There are over 400 types of rum on offer and many rare and vintage varieties stored in the 'Vault'. The inventive use of rum varies from traditional Caribbean to classic prohibition era and tiki style.

I CAN FEEL SOME SWASHBUCKLING COMING ON.
The expert mixologists at the bar will have you swinging from the rafters with libations like 'The Expedition' – dark rum and bourbon, chicory coffee liqueur and a touch of honey, vanilla and cinnamon. If you pay extra for the drink, you can make off with the tiki-style mug that it's served in. AAAArrrggh.

36

NICK OTTO © ALAMY

Sum Yi Tai / Singapore

THAT'S A BIT OF A MOUTHFUL.
Conceptualised to pay tribute to the glory and glamour of 1980s-90s Hong Kong, Sum Yi Tai (which means 'third wife' in Cantonese) is certainly full of kitsch and colour.

I LOVE KITSCH AND COLOUR.
Well you'll love this. There are fake roast ducks hung like artworks on display beside the downstairs tapas bar. There are crimson lamps and black stools and even a Chinese dragon suspended from the ceiling. The decor creates an underground gangland vibe and is dramatically fun. The ambiance sets high expectations for food and drink.

SPEAKING OF WHICH...
The downstairs tapas bar menu is full of Cantonese dishes like salmon skin with salted egg yolk and lime zest, or crispy baby octopus with barbecue sauce. The serene second-floor dining room menu has filling delights like claypot beef brisket with white daikon or pan-fried minced pork with crispy salted fish.

AND DRINKING?
Speciality cocktails have cheesy romantic stories attached – the 'Date a Gangster' evokes the tale of a woman blinded by love, who will do anything for her man – whisky, Drambuie liqueur, triple sec, lemon juice and dates. Ready to swoon?

Tales & Spirits / Amsterdam

WHAT'S THE DEAL?

Here's how you do a classic cocktail bar: smooth bartenders in suspenders and skinny ties, crystal chandeliers overhanging a dark wooden bar, a cocktail menu that mixes the old-school with some new flavour combinations. Oh, and great food.

I COULD DO WITH SOME NEW COCKTAILS.

There are house specials like 'The Fallen Lady' – a sweet ode to the women who work the red-light district in which the bar is located – vodka, dark chocolate liqueur, raspberry syrup, lemon juice and bitters; and the zingy 'What If?' – a twist on the standard daiquiri with rum, fresh lime, and pineapple-and-ginger shrub. Many of the cocktails are served in the bar's collection of vintage, rare and antique glasses – a nice touch.

I DON'T THINK I'M GOING TO STOP AT ONE.

If there's any truth to the notion that quality spirits mean no hangover, you'll be fine. If it's bogus, keep the next day free for horizontal recovery.

YOU MENTIONED FOOD?

T&S is almost as serious about food as it is about drinks. Dishes like scallop ceviche or confit quail legs might help you avoid a hangover. If that notion isn't smoke and mirrors too.

17-2 NORTH XIANG YANG RD,
SHANGHAI, CHINA
WWW.YUANLOUNGE.COM

Yuan Oyster & Cocktail Bar / Shanghai

NIGHTLIFE CENTRAL!

We can't hide the fact that there are a lot of good bars in Shanghai. But seen one hotel bar, seen 'em all.

ARE YOU PROMISING SOMETHING DIFFERENT?

Yuan is refreshing, in a number of ways. For one, it's locally owned and run. And it takes its drinks seriously while also bringing a bit of Chinese flair and flavour to the party.

CHINESE FLAIR AND FLAVOUR?

There are lanterns, Chinese art, random knick-knacks. Kind of kitsch, but brought together in a way that doesn't feel forced.

And the cocktails – expect clever blends of Western and Chinese spirits. You'll certainly find something delicious that you've never heard of, let alone imbibed.

FOR EXAMPLE?

Try the 'Chongming Peach': with peach vodka, Chongming rice wine and lemon, it's fruity, sweet, earthy and zingy. Don't forget the oysters – the bar takes pride in its fresh molluscs.

I THINK YOU LIKE THIS PLACE.

Shanghai is a crazy, gigantic, awesome city. This little bar will help you feel right at home. See you there.

A'brewin' // Craft beer bars

IMPASSE DE LA FIDÉLITÉ 4A,
BRUSSELS, BELGIUM
WWW.DELIRIUMCAFE.BE

Delirium Café / Brussels

I HAVE A FEELING THAT THIS MIGHT INVOLVE AN ALE.

This is definitely one for the beer lovers. Recognised by the Guinness Book of Records as having the largest selection of beers in the world, the beer menu at the Delirium Café is over 240 pages long. In this, there are approximately 2000 Belgian beers and another 500 or so from over 75 countries around the world.

THERE'S A DEFINITE THEME GOING ON.

Oh yes. Peer inside and you'll find beer-related paraphernalia scattered throughout too.

I DON'T KNOW WHERE TO START.

If you can get a word in with the bar staff they're more than willing to make suggestions based on your likes and dislikes, but the bar is often packed so it pays to do some research before you arrive. The finest Belgian Lambic and Abbey beers are a good place to start.

IT'S INCREDIBLY BUSY, CAN I GET A SEAT ANYWHERE?

If the original bar is too crowded, just head upstairs to the Delirium Tap House where there'll be a choice of 27 draft beers on tap.

2505 3RD ST, DOGPATCH,
SAN FRANCISCO, USA
WWW.MAGNOLIASMOKESTACK.COM

Magnolia Brewing Company / San Francisco

IS THERE ANYTHING BEER CAN'T DO?
No, it can do anything and everything. Let us prove it to you.

YOU'LL BE PREACHING TO THE CONVERTED, BUT SURE, GIVE IT TO ME.
Magnolia Brewing Company cut its teeth on the smaller, wildly popular Magnolia Gastropub and Brewery on Haight St before opening this larger joint in 2014, and the expertise shows.

LET ME GUESS: IT'S IN A FACTORY.
You are 11 kinds of right! Housed in a former can factory, it's got reclaimed wooden tables, exposed piping and a double-height wall of liquor. And there's beer; almost 20 different draft and cask craft beers: IPAs, brown ales and wheat, all meticulously crafted and served with pride and extensive knowledge about the brewing process... along with a serious list of small-batch whiskeys.

YOU'VE HIT EVERY CRAFT BEER BUZZWORD THERE.
And we haven't even mentioned the menu. Would it surprise you to know it serves barbecue? Of course not, because what's better than beer and barbecue? The restaurant, Smokestack, serves beer-side favourites: brisket, Wagyu ribs, smoked chicken and hot pastrami. If it ain't broke...don't fix it.

PETRITEGI BIDEA, 20115 ASTIGARRAGA,
GIPUZKOA, SPAIN
WWW.PETRITEGI.COM

Petritegi Tolare Sagardotegia / San Sebastián

YOU'VE LOST ME.

A *sargardotegia* is a cider house. You're near San Sebastián in the Basque country of Spain. You're about to keep the doctor away with a healthy dose of apple.

OOH, MEDICINAL DRINKING. I'M A FAN.

Let's not overmedicate, but it's easy to imagine getting drawn into a rustic life of addictive simple pleasures.

I'VE ALWAYS WANTED TO STOMP ON APPLES.

You might get lucky and arrive as the apples begin their transformation – but leave it to the experts (they've been doing this here for almost 500 years) and instead sample the cider, freshly tapped from one of the many barrels. Think dry, crisp, complex, perfect with salt-cod omelette or cured meats.

I THINK I MIGHT BE IN LOVE.

It's the right feeling. Some places get it right; genuine hospitality, a great story, a deeply satisfying experience – Petritegi delivers it all. And did we talk about the Basque snacks?

THAT'S IT, I'M GOING TO REHABILITATE HERE.

Hope you feel better soon.

5TH FL, OD KOTVA, NÁMĚSTÍ REPUBLIKY 656/8,
PRAGUE, CZECH REPUBLIC
WWW.T-ANKER.CZ

T-Anker / Prague

TELL ME ALL.
On the roof of the Kotva department store in Prague's Old Town is this gem of a bar. What makes it so? It's one of those special places that manages to be all things to all people.

THAT'S REFRESHING.
It gets better. There's a huge, sunny, outdoor terrace with stunning views over the cobbled streets and the ancient rooftops of the old town, stretching all the way to the castle.

SPEAKING OF REFRESHING ...
There are approximately 100 different varieties of beer to choose from including a weekly rotating roster of tapped beer and a choice of another 60 local and international bottled beers. A meat-heavy menu (think steaks and burgers) complements the beer list, though there are also lighter snacks like spicy chicken wings or Caesar salad. There's even a kids' playground to keep little folks entertained.

PLEASE SHOW ME THE DOOR.
Here's a fun fact about getting through the front door at T-Anker: you have to access the rooftop via a glass elevator that rises slowly from the ground all the way up the outside of the building. Cool, hey?

PETR BONEK © ALAMY

Tørst / New York City

WHAT IS THAT LINE THROUGHT THE 'O' SUPPOSED TO MEAN?

Er....

GO ON.

'Er.' Like the 'er' in 'fern'. It's a letter and no Scandinavian can do without it. Here it is a harbinger of the décor and style. It also means 'thirst' in Danish.

UM... BUT I'M IN BROOKLYN.

Don't worry, my friend. Décor is one thing, but the sheer crafty focus on beer taken to the nth degree will have your Brooklyn-hipster radar singing out loud.

I DO LIKE A BEER.

This is the place then. With 20-odd draft beers available, each cooled to a unique temperature, it truly is beer nirvana. Or maybe that should be beer-valhalla.

IT'S SOUNDING A LITTLE INTIMIDATING.

This bar doesn't let extreme beer-nerd-dom get in the way of hospitality. Geek out or go your own way. You'll be fine.

IS THERE A SIGNATURE BEER?

The list is ever-changing, although the bar being co-owned by Evil Twin brewer Jeppe Jarnit-Bjergsø (there's one of those 'o's!) means a jar of an Evil Twin brew should be perfect.

© SIGNE BIRCK

Shh! // Hidden bars

Area 51 Top Secret Party Facility / Boracay

SO WHAT'S THE DEAL?

Apart from having one of the greatest club names ever, Area 51 (low voice) is the only underground party spot on the island of Boracay.

OOH, MYSTERIOUS. WHEN'S IT ON?

Its schedule is appropriately linked to the phases of the moon, ie there are full-moon and black-moon parties each month, as well as others in the high season.

MUST GET PRETTY BUSY, THEN.

These are some of the biggest parties around, 400 to 500 strong, particularly on special holidays like Halloween and New Year's Eve, and they last from midnight to sunrise.

WHAT ON EARTH WOULD I BE DOING FROM MIDNIGHT TO SUNRISE?

Expect food stalls, music, tribal drumming, fire dancing and the usual refreshments, in the unique island experience that is Boracay. The wildly hedonistic vibe is like Nevada's shape-shifting Burning Man festival, occupying the space between religion, cult and wild party spirit. This is all if you can find your way, of course. Look for the sign on the fence in front of the Dead Forest, on the road by Lugutan Beach. Aliens welcome.

Aux Deux Amis / Paris

I WALKED BY AND IT LOOKED LIKE A SIMPLE CAFE.
True, it looks modest with tiled floors, Formica tables and
wooden chairs, but don't judge it by the unassuming facade.

WELL, WHY GO THERE?
I think the words we're looking for are 'real deal'.

NO TOURISTS THEN?
Apart from you of course. Seriously, this is exactly the kind of
place every visitor to Paris dreams of finding themselves in. An
authentic, retro little neighbourhood wine bar packed with
lively locals and animated visitors. Enjoying *vin naturel* by the

glass with tasty classic tapas plates like beef carpaccio, white
asparagus and grilled sardines.

HMMM, SOUNDS DECEPTIVELY SIMPLE.
No deception, that's the magic. This place brings together a
combination of unpretentious elements to create a uniquely
French atmosphere. The wine list is entirely natural and
sourced directly from local producers; the menu is driven by
quality ingredients in both bistro and tapas style; service is
convivial and brisk and the clientele are chic and cheerful. Aux
Deux Amis delivers a night of beautiful wine, great food and
joyful company and you can't ask for more than that.

CALLE 17 NO 302, BTWN CALLES 2 & 4,

VEDADA, HAVANA, CUBA

WWW.MADRIGALBARCAFE.WORDPRESS.COM

Café Madrigal / Havana

I ALWAYS THINK OF HEMINGWAY WHEN I THINK OF CUBA. AND CIGARS.

Well there's no cigars, but it's bohemian, artsy, and quirkily decorated with cinematic paraphernalia, harking back to the former film-directing career of the bar's owner, Rafael Rosales. So Hemingway-esque for sure. In fact, this was once Rafael's home until he decided to turn it into a bar.

TURNING ONE'S HOME INTO A BAR SOUNDS LIKE A GREAT IDEA.

It would have its upside, sure. In this case, the location can be hard to find – it's in a residential neighbourhood on the top floor of a gorgeous two-storey art nouveau building. Listen out for animated conversations drifting over the rooftops.

WITH WHOM WILL I BE SHARING THIS HOME?

Madrigal attracts young Cuban intellectual types who enjoy intense conversations over their mojitos (it's a classic bar list with the usual suspects). In recent years tourists have joined in with the locals to share the live music (on most nights) and tasty tapas plates. Try the *tostones* (fried plantains) with cheese or the *empanadas del Madrigal* with a plum sauce on the side.

MERCAT DE LA BOQUERIA, LA RAMBLA 91,
BARCELONA, SPAIN
WWW.ELQUIMDELABOQUERIA.COM

El Quim de la Boqueria / Barcelona

WHAT HAVE I GOT MYSELF INTO HERE?

Literally, you've landed in a market, the Mercat de la Boqueria, famed for its fresh seafood, fruit and vegetables, and regional ham. This small tapas bar/restaurant is right in the bustle of it all. The sights and smells of the surrounding fresh produce create an inspiring and mouth-watering atmosphere that feels quintessentially Spanish.

THAT'S NOT USUALLY MY KIND OF DRINKING ESTABLISHMENT.

We know it's being a bit cheeky to say that the reason you should go to this bar is for the food. But there it is. The food is the star of this small 18-stool establishment and you're just lucky to be able to down an alcoholic beverage at the same time.

WELL, FOOD IT IS. WHAT'S ON THE MENU?

There's a mix of traditional tapas like *patatas bravas* and Catalan specialities like butifarra sausage with white beans and mayonnaise. Chef Quim is a master of his trade and serves up daily specials, cooked fresh for you while you wait. The *huevos con chipirones* – fried eggs with baby squid, garlic and chilli – is something close to a signature dish and should not to be missed.

542 W 27TH ST, BTWN TENTH & ELEVENTH AVES,

NEW YORK CITY, USA

WWW.MCKITTRICKHOTEL.COM/GALLOW-GREEN

50

Gallow Green / NYC

WHAT A DAY! I WALKED A HUNDRED BLOCKS.

If you could step off NY's hot and stinky summer streets into an overgrown haven of greenery on a hotel rooftop, well, would that make you feel better?

ISN'T IT JUST ANOTHER ROOFTOP BAR?

This isn't a rooftop all about slick views of the Manhattan skyline, instead it's more like a secret neighbourhood allotment, raised off the street and scattered with wooden tables and chairs and odd little turn-of-the-century curios, all tucked into leafy, sun-dappled, vine-lined corners – ripe for long, lazy conversations under the setting summer sun.

ALL THIS SUNSHINE IS MAKING ME THIRSTY.

The cocktail list reads like something from an old English garden party: the 'June & Jennifer', for example, brims with Bols Genever gin, chartreuse, strawberry, mint, lime and champagne. Then there are the large punch bowls to share (think Pernod absinthe, Delord Armagnac, sparkling mineral water and lemon oleo) – they'd make Gatsby proud.

WHAT'S ON OUR METAPHORICAL PICNIC RUG?

Bowls of salads and boards of pickled bites, terrines and cheeses keep the locally-grown, community aesthetic of this garden-style oasis buzzing.

MALABIA 1764, PALERMO,
BUENOS AIRES, ARGENTINA
TEL: +54-11-4831-0519

The Harrison Speakeasy / Buenos Aires

PLEASE NO, NOT ANOTHER SPEAKEASY?

Of the speakeasies that have popped up like pimples on the face of major cities in the last decade this place puts most to shame. It is one of the most genuine and one of the best.

I'VE BEEN BURNED BY THIS SPEAKEASY THING BEFORE.

Haven't we all. But give a gangster a chance. Just getting inside the front door, or at least the first front door, is an adventure. There are passwords and secret entrances and a strictly enforced photography ban (well, no-one had smartphones in the 1920s now did they?).

SOUNDS LIKE A LOT OF RIGMAROLE FOR A COCKTAIL.

While some speakeasies make the secrecy feel like a chore the Harrison turns the clandestineness into an exciting and exclusive game. Once past the sushi shop and through the vault-like door, you'll find a dark and ornate wooden bar, dimly lit lamps and even an old piano.

I'M EXHAUSTED.

Prepare to be refreshed. The expert bartenders are magicians, concocting flavours tailored to your personal taste – even Al Capone would be impressed.

The Jerry Thomas Project / Rome

I'M IN ITALY AND I'M GOING TO A BAR CALLED 'JERRY'?

That's 'Jerry Thomas' thank you. And why not? It's named after Jerry Thomas, the author of the original *Bartender's Guide* published in 1862. We're in speakeasy territory ...

AHHH ... SPEAKEASY RULES THEN.

There are a few, like no photos, cash only and no vodka. The password palaver you're expected to go through to get into so many speakeasies is a relatively easy code to crack here: just look up the website (though most of the website is in Italian, this crucial bit of info is translated into English).

WHAT SECRET WONDERLAND AWAITS?

Once inside it's all roaring '20s chic, leather lounges and candle-lit tables. The waistcoated bartenders are happy to please.

WAS JERRY THOMAS REALLY ITALIAN?

No, American. Consider it a sign that the mixology masters here take their knowledge of cocktails seriously. Despite the penchant for classic concoctions you can have a bespoke cocktail on request to cater to your mood and personal tastes. It's an exercise in professionalism. There are home-style bar snacks available too.

70

Past lives // Historical bars

Cave Bar / Petra

THIS PLACE DOES NOT
LOOK ANYTHING LIKE MY LOCAL.

Like never before, you have been transported to a very different time zone. Occupying a 2000-year-old Nabataean rock tomb, this Petra drinking hole is the world's oldest bar. Pretty impressive.

ALL VERY PEACEFUL, I IMAGINE.

Well, not exactly. The blue-lit Cave Bar hotspot has been known to stay open until 4am on busy summer nights. Don't be put off by the loud music you find at the entrance, though: the noise stops there.

HM. ANYTHING ELSE YOU NEED TO TELL
ME THAT I SHOULD KNOW ABOUT?

Commune with the spirits, alcoholic or otherwise, and you'll soon get a flavour of Petra you hadn't bargained on (not least the 26% tax and service charge!).

I'VE WORKED UP AN APPETITE
JUST THINKING ABOUT IT.

The menu includes delicious comfort food such as potato wedges and fish and chips you may feel you've earned after a day's exercise in Petra. It might not be gourmet Middle Eastern fare, but with a backdrop like this, crisps would almost do.

Gordon's Wine Bar / London

ARE YOU SURE THIS IS A BAR?

I see your point: the little entrance gives just a hint at the truly subterranean drinking scene inside. But descend the rickety wooden staircase and you find a cavernous, candle-lit basement, stacked with wooden tables under a curved-stone ceiling.

IT MUST BE QUIET AS A MORGUE.

There's a buzzing hubbub of happy punters. It's super snug and wonderfully atmospheric, although if you're claustrophobic or just enjoy natural light with your wine there is outdoor seating on the side of Watergate Walk.

SO GORDON'S PRIDES ITSELF ON WINE?

Gordon's promotes itself as being London's oldest wine bar (established in 1890) and there is an impressive international wine list to back it up. Also, there is a specials board promising a range of limited edition wines from private domains.

WHAT CAN I EAT?

What goes better with wine than cheese? Gordon's has a mouth-watering array of more than 20 cheeses (international and local) to choose from and each board is expertly matched with wine. Beyond the cheese boards there are larger pub lunches, a Sunday roast and some tapas in the evenings.

TIM E WHITE © ALAMY

213 UNION ST,
ABERDEEN, SCOTLAND, UK
WWW.THEGRILLABERDEEN.CO.UK

The Grill / Aberdeen

I'M FEELING A WEE BIT THIRSTY.
That's how it starts. Then you find yourself in the heart of Aberdeen, Scotland's sparkling city, being served whisky and, um, well whisky.

SO THIS PLACE IS GOING TO BE FULL OF MIDDLE- TO LATE-AGED MEN DROOLING OVER DRAMS?
Ah yes, but the bar welcomes all comers. Even women.

WHAT DOES THAT MEAN?
Despite being open since around 1870 women were only allowed in the front door after 1975 and it took another 20-odd years for them to put a women's toilet in place!

GOOD TO SEE THEY'VE CAUGHT UP WITH THE TIMES.
This is actually a lovely, warm place with a striking traditional long-bar counter running the length of the room, and those behind it are genuinely friendly and knowledgeable.

GO ON THEN, TELL US ABOUT THE WHISKY.
There are over 500 different malt whiskies, Scottish and international. And a range of very old and rare single malts from distilleries that no longer produce – this is the only place in the world where you can sample them over the counter.

Sean's Bar / Athlone

I WAS WONDERING WHEN IRELAND WOULD COME CALLING.

If you were to astrally project yourself to the spiritual home of enjoying a drop, you'd most definitely be in Ireland, right? So here we are.

RIGHT, SKIP THE ASTRAL PROJECTION, I'M THERE.

Well where you are then is the oldest drinking hole in Ireland, and possibly the world (the jury's out). Bits and pieces of the building allow for a pretty impressive 'Est 900 AD' plaque. Read that again...900 AD. ... Exactly, words fail.

SHHH, I'M DRINKING IT IN.

OK. While you're musing, blow the fear of cliche and take a pint of Guinness. That rich, warming brew really is the done thing.

WHEN IN ROME. DID YOU REALLY SAY 900 AD?

Hospitality began here in, yes, 900 AD, with Luain, an innkeeper who helped travellers cross the ford. By our count that's a lot of beer, mead, ale, Guinness and whiskey. The original walls are still in there somewhere, though it's a more contemporary-looking (last 200 years say!) place now. Find the fireplace (or beer garden) and let your spirit be your guide.

VII KAZINCZY UTCA 14,
BUDAPEST, HUNGARY
WWW.SZIMPLA.HU

Szimpla Kert / Budapest

I HAVE NO IDEA WHAT TO EXPECT.
Szimpla Kert is simply the finest example of Budapest's *romkocsma*, or ruin bars.

WHAT'S A RUIN BAR?
Ruin bars sprung up in Budapest's post-communist landscape among many of the crumbling old buildings that the city could no longer afford to maintain. An enterprising few saw an opportunity for cheap rent and went ahead and made some of the buildings structurally sound in order to turn the spaces into places for people to meet, drink and generally to have a good time.

WILL I PERCH MY BEER ON A BROKEN-DOWN EDIFICE?
One of the most delightful things about ruin bars and Szimpla Kert in particular is the juxtaposition between the dilapidated exterior and the eclectically assembled, colourfully lit, rambling warmth of the interior. Chairs, tables, cars, bikes are scattered in the nooks and crannies and around the open-air courtyard.

SOUNDS LIKE A GREAT HOUSE PARTY.
Throw in some good tunes, a mix of craft and regular beers on tap and a globally inspired menu peppered with some Hungarian specialities like stew with Mangalica sausage, and you have the best house party you've ever been to.

Rhythm // Music & party bars

8TH FL, STIKLAL CADDESI 163,
ISTANBUL, TURKEY
WWW.360ISTANBUL.COM

360 Istanbul / Istanbul

360 SAYS 'VIEWS' TO ME.

Istanbul is one of those cities that begs to be seen from a height. The beautiful Bosphorus cuts a swathe through the mix of ancient and modern buildings, many of which are lit up at night. 360 Istanbul gives you one of the best platforms to soak in the stunning surrounds.

AND THE VIEW INSIDE?

Music, food and cocktails. How's that look? And 360 Istanbul runs a rotating roster of DJs and live music which draws in a boisterous crowd of the city's young, hipster set.

NOW I'M FEELING THE FULL 360.

Settle in then. The food is modern Turkish mezze with an international twist, for example bulgur kofte dumplings with pistachios. Or maybe a prawn ceviche salad with avocado and lime.

SO THIRSTY...

There's a drinks menu stacked with red and white Turkish wines and quite a few French bubblies. Cocktails won't astound or surprise and generally run the standard gamut. Settle in with a glass of Turkish pinot and get back into enjoying the view.

Blue Frog Lounge / Mumbai

SO WHY AM I GOING THERE?

Walking into the Bluefrog is like walking into an alien's spaceship, or maybe it's more like an enormous beehive-turned-nightclub... in any case, you get the picture – it is entirely otherworldly.

HOW SO?

Large, floating metal discs are suspended from the ceiling and there are cylindrical booth seats dotted like giant honeycomb around the bar floor. The Bluefrog Lounge's surfaces are smooth and fluid, and the whole place pulses with psychedelic lighting.

SOUNDS CRAZY – WHAT'S THE DEAL WITH THIS PLACE?

It's a music venue as much as a bar with a constantly rotating line-up of local and international artists, usually with an electronic edge. In fact they love music so much here that there's actually a recording studio as part of the complex.

CAN I GO FOR A DRINK AND A BITE TO EAT?

Yes, there's an extensive drinks list including a set of pretty standard cocktails. They won't tell you what's in the 'Blue Frog' except to say that it's potent. Perhaps order a round of fried bar snacks as insurance.

707 E PINE ST,
SEATTLE, USA
WWW.LINDASTAVERN.COM

Linda's Tavern / Seattle

I HAVE THAT FEELING AGAIN,
THE ONE THAT SAYS I'M COMING HOME.

I have a feeling you're right – this is a dive bar, and it's you all over. That is to say, it's one of the best dive bars around but it does what it says on the tin, so high heels and dinner jackets be gone. You can't be drinking shots and jugs of beer in that kind of get-up.

SO WHAT CAN I EXPECT FROM THIS DIVE BAR?

To begin with you can expect a damn good time. It's one of Seattle's original dive bars and has garnered iconic status over the years, not least because this bar was reportedly the last place Kurt Cobain was seen alive. It buzzes with a crowd of mostly indie rockers and hipsters. You've got all you need at Linda's, with a pool table, a jukebox and an outside patio that gets completely packed out on sunny days.

I'LL BE ABLE TO GET A BURGER HERE, RIGHT?

Despite the disapproving looks from the enormous taxidermied buffalo head above the bar, Linda's does serve a gamut of fried meat products. We've heard the chicken fried steak is the pick from the popular brunch menu.

PLAC TEATRALNY I,
WARSAW, POLAND
WWW.OPERACLUB.PL

Opera Club / Warsaw

IS THIS THE GRANDEST KARAOKE BAR EVER?
Remind me to never go to karaoke with you. It's a bar in the basement of the national opera house in Warsaw, Poland.

BASEMENT? DIVE?
You are here to experience sumptuous elegance and sensuous decadence. This bar was reportedly once used by Polish royalty to engage in clandestine love liaisons.

THIS ALL SOUNDS VERY SEXY.
The Opera Club tends to take its sexy seriously – meaning: the swanky dress code is very much strictly enforced. Make sure to scrub up before attempting to get into the venue.

IS IT WORTH ALL THE EFFORT?
If you make it past the door you'll descend into a labyrinthine set of disused tunnels under the home of the Polish National Opera, the Grand Theatre. Winding your way through rooms and semi-private nooks, you'll eventually find yourself on the dance floor, packed with 300 of your closest friends.

HOW SHOULD I KICK OFF MY LAVISH EVENING?
The 'Opera Iced Tea' should set you up, with its vodka, gin, rum, tequila, triple sec, lemon and sugar. Are you singing yet?

46-8 MITCHAM RD, WANDSWORTH,
LONDON, UK
WWW.TOOTINGTRAMANDSOCIAL.CO.UK

Tooting Tram & Social / London

THIS SOUNDS VERY JOLLY.

Here is a bar that might just be all things to all people. And jolly to boot. You'll love it.

ALL THINGS TO ALL PEOPLE SOUNDS LIKE A BAR RECIPE FOR DISASTER.

This may be true, but here, it works. Drop in for a pre-drink yoga session, lose your mind to one of the DJ sets, unwind post-work with mates or sing your lungs out at an open-mic.

BLURGH...OPEN-MIC.

Check their calendar of events and do yoga instead.

MAYBE I'LL DANCE, THANKS.

Go crazy. The place is fitted with a high-end sound system and, along with a late-night licence, your moves will bring the roof down. (Speaking of the roof... did we mention that the Tooting Tram & Social has 75-ft ceilings? This old tram shed was built for big!).

I MIGHT BECOME A REGULAR.

If you're in town, why wouldn't you? It's all about a good time. Drinks are plenty and varied enough (but this isn't a cocktail paradise), and the atmosphere says comfort and fun. It really is jolly good.

Heaven // Bars in paradise

Baba Nest / Phuket

THIS SOUNDS VERY COSY.

It is, cosy and luxurious. It's part of the Sri Panwa resort, on the coast of Phuket in Thailand's south.

OF ALL THE THAI BEACH RESORTS, WHY AM I HERE?

Do it. Most people go so they can ooh and ahh at the spectacular sunset. Truthfully, it's pretty special – even more so when you're looking at it with a cocktail in hand, on a giant comfy cushion. The bar's rooftop platform hovers, like an airborne wooden jetty, over the beach below, with nearly 360° views of the island's beautiful surrounds. Oh and if that's not enough, the whole podium is encircled by an infinity pool.

SOUNDS LIKE IT MAY BE PACKED WITH PEOPLE POINTING THEIR PHONES TOWARDS THE SUN?

We can't lie, there will be a few happy snappers, but there's limited capacity at Baba Nest so only the special 40 or so with a reservation can elbow each other out of the way when capturing lifetime memories.

WHAT HAPPENS WHEN THE PHOTO OPPORTUNITIES ARE EXHAUSTED?

That's when you'll see everyone sitting peacefully, languidly chatting, legs outstretched, with blissed-out expressions on their sun-kissed faces.

Hula Hula / Hvar

SERIOUSLY, IF I HAVE TO HULA HOOP I'M NOT GOING.
Relax: this is beachside bar-action at its finest. There's definitely an energetic vibe, a pumping dance floor in the evenings and a throng of beautiful people dancing. But that's optional.

AND IF I DON'T FEEL LIKE DANCING?
Daylight hours mean laid-back drinks under the sun, water at your feet. You should probably think about jumping in and building up a thirst.

OK, I'M COMING AROUND TO THE IDEA.
Well, it's about time. This bar is all about holiday mode.

Lounge around from breakfast, meandering through the menu, enjoying a cocktail, priming yourself for evening shenanigans.

WHAT COCKTAIL SHOULD I RECLINE WITH?
You're on holiday, no-one's judging you: get the 'Hula Hula' cocktail. Don't ask what's in it, just go with its bright pink wonder and cool fruity goodness.

I'M STARTING TO FEEL LIKE DANCING.
By sunset a DJ will be setting the mood and the crowd will reach epic proportions. You'll be a dancing fool before you can say 'Pass me the hula hoop.'

Rick's Café / Negril

IT'S IN JAMAICA? I'M IN.
Well... we do aim to please. But wait, there's more to come from Rick's Café.

WHAT ELSE COULD THERE BE?
The cliff diving, the sunsets, the rowdy crowds of sun-kissed revellers, the tropical cocktails, the live reggae every night. Those are some of the reasons.

OK, ALL OF IT, BUT CLIFF DIVING?
You heard correctly. Locals and tourists take the plunge off the surrounding cliffs near Rick's. Locals expect a tip but tourists just do it for bragging rights. It makes for a fun sight for patrons at the bar.

I THINK I'D RATHER STICK TO SOLID GROUND AND SOAK UP THE REGGAE AND TROPICAL COCKTAILS.
Fair enough; there's certainly less risk involved and when the sun starts to set and the reggae is pumping it's easy to see why Rick's has gained its legendary status. Join the sprawl of mostly young and lively clientele for a jug of Rick's signature rum punch; tuck into a giant plate of buttered, broiled lobster and let the happiness wash right over you.

Rock Bar / Bali

I LOVE ROCK!
Wrong rock. This is geological perfection.

PERFECTION?
Look at the location: cosseted by the luxury Ayana Resort and Spa on what's known as the 'sunset' coast of Bali's little almost-island offshoot, Jimbaran. Exotic perfection, tick.

WHERE'S THE ROCK?
Seaspray sprinkles the drinks as they're prepared for patrons from this stunning rock-hewn bar. The literal proximity to the water and tropical sunset makes for a sensational experience.

SOUNDS JUST A LITTLE TOO GOOD TO BE TRUE.
The hyperbole around this bar's setting is entirely warranted but the drawback is that it's guests of the resort who get the inside track on the queue to get in. So, if you're not a resort guest then the wait for a wave-side seat can be tedious.

DRINKS, FOOD?
Does it really matter what you eat or drink when you have a front-row seat for the sun setting on the Pacific Ocean? It does? Well, luckily the bar doesn't just rest on its rocky laurels. There's a serious list of basic-spirit cocktails and a greatest hits list of globally-inspired bar snacks.

Soggy Dollar Bar / British Virgin Islands

I CAN ONLY GUESS THAT I'M ABOUT TO GET WET.

It's a distinct possibility. Actually, it's a certainty. This is beachside drinking at its best. Pick a tropical-paradise cliche and apply here – pristine white-sand beach; crystal clear waters; swaying palm trees with hammocks gently rocking in the breeze...

CLICHE OR NOT, I'M IN.

You'd be crazy if you weren't. But that certainty comment? The only way to get to the Soggy Dollar is to charter a boat and swim ashore from the closest mooring point. Dry off your soggy currency and order the signature drink, the 'Painkiller'.

WHY WOULD I NEED A PAINKILLER?
THIS PLACE SOUNDS PERFECT.

Could be a hint at how you may be feeling the day after a trip to the Soggy Dollar...the 'Painkiller' is a heady mix of classic Caribbean flavours which include dark rum, cream of coconut and pineapple and orange juice.

I GUESS I SHOULD EAT SOMETHING.

Good idea. Choose from a selection of crowd-pleasing American-inspired meals with a Caribbean twist. Like the mahi fish sandwich, conch fritters, or the Caesar salad with jerk chicken.

Whimsy // Quirky bars

Baobab Tree Bar / Limpopo

SO WHY AM I GOING OFF THE BEATEN TRACK IN SOUTH AFRICA FOR A BAR?

It's a bar that's nested inside a baobab tree! Known as the widest tree in the world, and unquestionably a symbol of Africa itself. And how many 6000-year-old bars have you been into anyway?

BUT I GO TO A BAR TO DRINK, NOT FOR ARBOREAL INTERESTS.

Yes, good point; luckily time spent at Baobab Tree Bar will inevitably involve a stayover at the on-site accommodation, and a visit to the nearby nature reserves and national parks

— Kruger National Park is not too far away, one of the largest game reserves on the continent. Big Five? You bet.

BUT BACK TO THE BAR...

Right, the bar! Surroundings aside, this is a homespun, super-hospitable place to swap yarns with fellow travellers. And share a drink of course. You got the bit about it being in a 6000-year-old tree, right?

AND WHAT SHOULD I DRINK THERE?

You'd have to think a cleansing ale makes the most sense after a day of hiking or quad-biking through the surrounding forests.

SOUTH AFRICAN TOURISM © FLICKR

Bounce Ping Pong / London

THIS IS A BOOK ABOUT BARS, RIGHT?
Let me check the cover. Yep, that's right.

PING PONG? NOT A TYPICAL NIGHT OUT THEN...
No, nothing about this bar is average, from its location in a huge space under an office block to the speakeasy-style fit-out disguised with 17 ping-pong tables and draping red curtains.

IDENTITY CRISIS?
The fairy godmother of drinks waved her wand over a disused rec centre. Turning it into a grown-ups' playground with booze, and a ping-pong table from the 2012 Olympic Games.

I MIGHT NEED AN ELECTROLYTE SPORTS DRINK.
Its drinks menu is inspired by the history of the local area and by ping pong. Being close to the 18th-century home of gin production means a gin-heavy cocktail list. For some sporty action try the 'Ping Pong Show' – tequila, lemongrass, ginger, fresh lime and grapefruit bitters. It'll bounce around your palate like a light, zingy...ping-pong ball.

I'M EXHAUSTED.
Have your food delivered table-side so you can keep playing. Ping-ponged out? Grab some pizza, served Italian-style from the counter, and head upstairs to secure a 1950s booth seat.

Le Comptoir General / Paris

BONJOUR!

Oui, you've landed in Paris's 10th arrondissement.

I COULD BE ON THE CHAMPS-ÉLYSÉES!

Let me explain with a metaphor. Imagine bars are like girls – stay with me – then the quintessential Parisienne wine bar is the stylish, smart girl you thought was unattainable in high school. Le Comptoir Général, however, is the pot-smoking, vintage-clad, wryly enigmatic girl you really wanted to get to know.

SOUNDS INTRIGUING.

This is not the kind of bar you'd normally expect to find in

Paris – it's a little bit San Francisco, a little bit Barcelona, but it's full of hip, artistic Parisiennes. It's in an old barn and retains some of that feel, except it's now full of a jumble of furniture, artworks, African-inspired artefacts and draping greenery.

I DON'T IMAGINE I'LL NEED MY FINEST COCKTAIL DRESS TO DRINK HERE.

Come as you are. The ambience is chilled. You decide what you pay to get in and once in you can take your pick of entertainment – cocktails in the courtyard; something to eat at the cafeteria; a movie at the in-house cinema; or simply relaxing with an African beer and watching the action unfold.

MARKNADSVÄGEN 63,
JUKKASJÄRVI, SWEDEN
WWW.ICEHOTEL.COM

Ice Bar / Jukkasjärvi

THIS SOUNDS FAMILIAR.

This is the original ice bar. There are many ice bar incarnations around the world but this innovator in Jukkasjärvi, Sweden, remains the best.

WHAT CAN I EXPECT?

You can expect things to get a little chilly. Temperatures are maintained at -5°C in order to keep the spectacularly carved interior as pristine as possible. Each year the bar is resculpted into a new design by international artists and sculptors. Artists also contribute to the design of the special artists' suites of the adjoining Icehotel.

I'D LIKE A HOT TODDY.

Would you like ice with that?

IS EVERYTHING MADE OF ICE?

Yes, the stools, tables, chairs, lamps, and even the glasses the drinks are served in are carved out of ice, although the dancefloor mixes it up by being covered in a light drift of snow.

SOUNDS ROMANTIC!

If the bar manages to warm the cockles of your heart there's an ice chapel attached to the hotel that performs weddings in frozen surrounds.

STR AVRAM IANCU 29,
CLUJ-NAPOCA, ROMANIA
WWW.JOBENBISTRO.COM

Joben Bistro / Cluj-Napoca

WELL THIS SOUNDS VERY CLASSIC AND TASTEFUL.
Um... sort of. The fit-out is straight out of the pages of a Jules Verne novel. There are exposed copper pipes, mechanical gear-like contraptions, levers, cogs and clocks all mounted on the walls throughout the three different rooms. There's even a giant glowing zeppelin suspended from the ceiling.

IT SOUNDS LIKE AN EDGY AND DECIDEDLY UNCOMFORTABLE PLACE FOR A DRINK.
This must be where really good interior design and architecture comes in. Joben is no tacky theme bar and despite the distinct industrial stylings it's still a warm and inviting place to have a drink. There are chesterfield lounges, cosy wooden tables and chairs and the lighting is by turns gentle and curious. Behind the bar an almost neon green light frames the mounted liquors and industrial art.

IF IT WAS A TACKY THEME BAR, WHAT'D IT BE CALLED?
Steampunk Heaven.

WHAT DO STEAMPUNKERS EAT AND DRINK?
It seems they like French bistro-style food with a nod to Americana, in the form of burgers. And they appreciate a meticulous mixologist as much as the rest of us.

Museum HR Giger Bar / Gruyères

SOMETHING TELLS ME I'M ABOUT TO BE CREEPED OUT.

All those who have already sampled a cocktail inside the desiccated shell of a giant mythical reptile, please walk on.

ARE YOU FOR SURREAL?

We sure are. This spectacular bar is the brainchild of Swiss artist HR Giger whose biomechanical style inspired the Ridley Scott blockbuster movie, *Alien*. And alien it is. Gigantic vertebrae stretch across the ceiling of the cavernous space creating the impression of having been swallowed by a gigantic reptilian creature.

YOU'RE MESSING WITH ME.

Deadly serious. Seats are like semi-cocoons that encircle glass-topped tables held up by skulls and bones of various sizes and the floor is a mosaic of vertebrae inspired patterning. Every inch of space is modelled and moulded in the alien-like theme and makes for a totally unreal experience.

I'M SCARED TO ASK ABOUT DRINKS AND FOOD.

Don't be. The menu and drinks list is fairly standard and doesn't follow in the footsteps of the design aesthetic. In fact, one of their bar snacks is a cream-filled meringue... now that's weird!

1305 COMMERCIAL DR,
VANCOUVER, CANADA
WWW.STORMCROWTAVERN.COM

The Storm Crow Tavern / Vancouver

SO WHAT'S THE DEAL?

Knowing the difference between Narnia and Neverwhere is not a prerequisite for enjoying this smashing pub. But if you do, you'll certainly make new friends.

SO WHAT YOU'RE SAYING IS IT'S A BAR FOR GEEKS.

With displays of Dr Who memorabilia, steampunk ray guns, and a big screen that shows classic sci-fi, fantasy and horror films – yes, it's a celebration for proud nerds everywhere.

I DO LIKE TO MINGLE WITH LIKEMINDED PEEPS.

Well, then, look no further. There's plenty to keep everyone entertained and involved, including role-play books and a wall of board games for the so-inclined (if you know what Elfenland is, that means you).

SOUNDS LIKE THIRSTY WORK.

Beer geeks will be happy here too. There's a small but perfectly formed menu of British Columbian brews (as well as some knowingly named cocktails like 'Romulan Ale' and 'Release the Kraken'), which will definitely get the thumbs up from the discerning drinker. When hunger strikes, the grub you'll find is of the cheap-and-cheerful sandwiches and shepherd's pie variety.

About the authors

Ben Handicott once published travel pictorial and reference books, dreams about, writes about and sometimes even does, travel. His favourite bars free pour.

Kalya Ryan is a travel writer, editor and strong advocate for visiting your local bar, your far-flung bars, and all bars in between. But especially the far-flung bars that take you to places you haven't been before and introduce you to new and exciting drinking experiences. Though she'd never say no to a classic martini.

Index

North America

Oceania

South America

Published in May 2016 by Lonely Planet
Publications Pty Ltd
ABN 36 005 607 983
www.lonelyplanet.com
ISBN 978 1 76034 058 2
© Lonely Planet 2016
Printed in China
10 9 8 7 6 5 4 3 2 1

Written by Ben Handicott and Kalya Ryan

Managing Director, Publishing Piers Pickard
Associate Publisher Robin Barton
Commissioning Editor Jessica Cole
Art Direction Daniel Di Paolo
Layout Designer Hayley Warnham
Editor Bridget Blair
Picture Researcher Christina Webb
Print Production Larissa Frost, Nigel Longuet
Cover image Sivan Askayo

Lonely Planet offices
AUSTRALIA
Level 2 & 3, 551 Swanston Street,
Carlton 3053, Victoria, Australia
Phone 03 8379 8000
Email talk2us@lonelyplanet.com.au

USA
150 Linden St, Oakland, CA 94607

Phone 510 250 6400
Email info@lonelyplanet.com

UNITED KINGDOM
240 Blackfriars Road, London SE1 8NW
Phone 020 3771 5100
Email go@lonelyplanet.co.uk

Although the authors and Lonely Planet have
taken all reasonable care in preparing this
book, we make no warranty about the accuracy
or completeness of its content and, to the
maximum extent permitted, disclaim all liability
from its use.

Paper in this book is certified against the Forest
Stewardship Council™ standards. FSC™ promotes
environmentally responsible, socially beneficial and
economically viable management of the world's forests.